This
Animal Tracks
book belongs to:

Can you **GUESS WHO** I am?

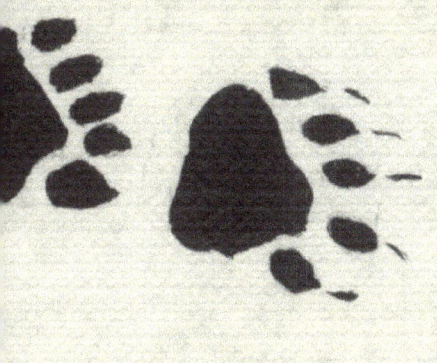
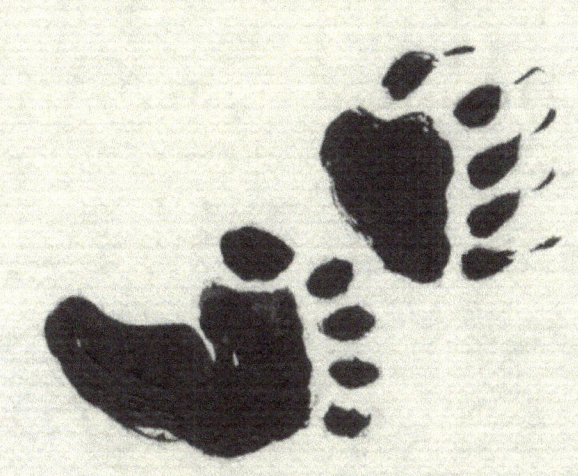

I left these paw tracks for you as a clue.

Hint: I am smaller than a kangaroo.

My coat is black and white.
Mostly, I roam around at night.

Can you GUESS WHO I am?

This is my tail.

If it goes up, RUN!

The smell of my spray is no fun.

Can you GUESS WHO I am now?

I am...

A SKUNK!

# Animal Tracks

Animal tracks are the marks left in the dirt, snow or mud when an animal walks over it.

How many animal tracks can you identify?

Look for tracks in your backyard or a park with your parent. Then try find out what kind of animal made them.

Now flip the book over to read Story 2.

Flip the book over to read Story 1

I am...

A RABBIT!

I leave lots of poops so you can follow my trail.

Can you
GUESS WHO
I am now?

These are my ears and that is my tail.

I am social and live with a group underground. Our warren is a large compound.

Hint: My fur is so soft that when people touch it they say, "Ooh!".

Can you GUESS WHO I am?

I have left these paw tracks for you as a clue.

This
Animal Tracks
book belongs to:

_____